In her debut collection *Where the Sky Opens: A Partial Cosmography*, Klein invites us, her "journey mates," to encounter a world more beautiful, complex and fragile than we often expect at the beginning of our faith histories. From the natural wonder of toads and lichens and mountain trails to the "wild, savory, perilous, graced" marriage relationship, these poems illuminate a sensitivity to life's lights and shadows through some of the most lush and visually intricate language I've read in years. Klein does not only write about, but *through* the loss of faith—and the love that redeems it—in "the kingdom emerging in guises we never knew."

—TANIA RUNYAN, author of *Second Sky*

What sinewy, mature poems these are, dynamic and packed with color! Laurie Klein's lines zero in on her life's crucial details that then enlarge, resonate and fill the frame of the reader's imagination. If asked, I'd say, "Dig in. Enjoy. This poet knows her way through words to things too vital to ignore."

—LUCI SHAW, Writer in Residence, Regent College, author of *Scape* and *Adventure of Ascent*

In *Where the Sky Opens*, Laurie Klein poses an implicit question of location. As it turns out, that sky opens in the reader's heart, crossed by flights of love and loss in poems that sing like red-winged blackbirds on the edge of a northern marsh. With a deftness of image and patience of faith, the poet reminds us to "let grief be, with every breath, a readied womb."

—PAUL J. WILLIS, author of *Say This Prayer into the Past*

Laurie Klein's first collection of poems is a glorious hymn of praise, inviting us into intimacy with things both known and unknown, earthy and sublime. Her language lifts you from the page into a poetic reverie and deeper reverence for life.

—CHRISTINE VALTERS PAINTNER, PhD, author of *The Artist's Rule: Nurturing Your Creative Soul with Monastic Wisdom*

I cannot remember the last time I read a poet with such burly thrumming love-addled music—dense and real and salty and singing, adamant and muscular and sharp—read any three of these poems and you will be more awake, which is what the best poetry is for. This book is that kind of poetry.

—BRIAN DOYLE, author of *Mink River*

WHERE THE SKY OPENS

The Poiema Poetry Series

Poems are windows into worlds; windows into beauty, goodness, and truth; windows into understandings that won't twist themselves into tidy dogmatic statements; windows into experiences. We can do more than merely peer into such windows; with a little effort we can fling open the casements, and leap over the sills into the heart of these worlds. We are also led into familiar places of hurt, confusion, and disappointment, but we arrive in the poet's company. Poetry is a partnership between poet and reader, seeking together to gain something of value—to get at something important.

Ephesians 2:10 says, "We are God's workmanship..." *poiema* in Greek— the thing that has been made, the masterpiece, the poem. The Poiema Poetry Series presents the work of gifted poets who take Christian faith seriously, and demonstrate in whose image we have been made through their creativity and craftsmanship.

These poets are recent participants in the ancient tradition of David, Asaph, Isaiah, and John the Revelator. The thread can be followed through the centuries—through the diverse poetic visions of Dante, Bernard of Clairvaux, Donne, Herbert, Milton, Hopkins, Eliot, R. S. Thomas, and Denise Levertov—down to the poet whose work is in your hand. With the selection of this volume you are entering this enduring tradition, and as a reader contributing to it.

—D.S. Martin
Series Editor

Where the Sky Opens

A Partial Cosmography

LAURIE KLEIN

CASCADE *Books* · Eugene, Oregon

WHERE THE SKY OPENS
A Partial Cosmography

The Poiema Poetry Series

Cascade Books
An Imprint of Wipf and Stock Publishers
199 W. 8th Ave., Suite 3
Eugene, OR 97401

www.wipfandstock.com

ISBN 13: 978-1-4982-3090-2

Cataloging-in-Publication data:

Laurie Klein.

Where the sky opens : a partial cosmography / Laurie Klein.

xiv + 82 p.; 23 cm

The Poiema Poetry Series

ISBN 13: 978-1-4982-3090-2

1. American Poetry—21st Century I. Title II. Series

PS3746.K312 2014

Manufactured in the USA.

For Will,
vagabond, dreamer, my heart's address

And for journey mates everywhere:
those who have gone on before,
and those still en route, detoured, stranded, or lost

. . . I will show them my wonders.
MICAH 7:15

Table of Contents

Preface | xiii
How to Live Like a Backyard Psalmist | 1

I. Portals

A Lone Bird, Balanced | 4
Exposed | 5
She Can Only Try to Compose Herself | 6
She Calls Him Dreamer | 7
Next Breath, Best Breath | 8
Blue as Devotion | 9
Jealous | 10
Warning | 11
Darkness Muscles between Us | 12
De Profundis | 13
Tethers | 14
Crash | 15
Burial at Sea | 16

II. Rhapsodies and Blues

Instrumental | 18
Right Brain Blues | 19
Ghost Stroke | 20
Unbelief | 21
Path Minder | 22
Some Instructions on Bending | 23
Washed Up | 24
En Route | 25

Table of Contents

Here on Earth | 26
Ms Demeanor | 27
Pipe Dream | 28
In Defense of the Occasional Gale | 29
In Thailand the Air Didn't Move | 30
The Back Forty | 31

III. Everyday Incarnations

Wayward | 34
Taffy and Cold Feet | 35
Delicate Arch | 36
Far and Away | 37
Bear | 38
Hunger's Plate of Secrets: Act I | 39
Reading Alone at Night | 40
Storm Toads: an Oracle | 41
Earthworks 301 | 42
Beloved Raptor | 43
Where the Sky Opens | 44
Jonah's Whale Addresses the Almighty | 45

IV. Tree, Temple, Wing

Lauds in a Pocket | 48
Re: Union | 49
I Try to Forgive Your Absence, Facing the Snake in the Kitchen | 50
Yes | 51
Sunday Shoes | 52
Love and Apostasy | 53
Picasso Might Have Seen It Like This | 54
In the Hothouse | 55
Suicide Trees | 56
Return Engagement | 57
Long Memories | 58
Catching Fire, or Notes to a Raku Vase | 59

V. Segue

Conclusions | 62
Hunger's Plate of Secrets: Act II | 63
Strung Out | 64
Every hurt place she begins to name | 65
Every Longing Implies a Beyond | 66
Altar | 67
Beginnings | 68
St. Kevin's Blackbird | 69
Migrations | 70
Bedrock | 71
Psalm 727 | 72

Afterward

Procrastination | 74
Roaming Charges | 75

Notes | 77
Acknowledgments | 79

Preface

Cosmography: "A general description of the world or of the universe" (Merriam-Webster).

Picture the bird's eye view with an occasional zoom. Flight paths fuel, or skew, our sight lines: My eyes, your eyes, take in a wild and partial cosmography.

The poems in *Where the Sky Opens* speak for, and about, journey mates crossing peculiar terrain. You'll find fellow travelers here, those who have gone on before, and those now en route, or detoured. Stranded. Lost. A partner jettisons lifelong faith; the pair redefines union.

How does truth unfold as the shared spiritual core of a relationship shatters?

Alternately exploring Nature or cocooning at home, the characters test the muscle of covenant, celebrate the erratic funny bone, and stretch the knotty sinews of grace.

Some days are limbo; others are matchless, breathtaking, out on a limb.

With love for this world and its Maker, and with deepening respect for seasons and crucial migrations—physical, relational, spiritual—I offer these poems as prayers for ever-expanding mercy, courage, and fidelity.

Laurie Klein
June 1, 2015

How to Live Like a Backyard Psalmist

Wear shoes with soles like meringue
and pale blue stitching so that
every day you feel ten years old.
Befriend what crawls.

Drink rain, hatless, laughing.

Sit on your heels before anything plush
or vaguely kinetic:
hazel-green kneelers of moss
waving their little parcels
of spores, on hair-trigger stems.

Hushed as St. Kevin cradling the egg,
new-laid, in an upturned palm,
tiptoe past a red-winged blackbird's nest.

Ponder the strange,
the charged, the dangerous:
taffeta rustle of cottonwood skirts,
Orion's owl, cruising at dusk,
thunderhead rumble. Bone-deep,
scrimshaw each day's secret.

Now, lighting the sandalwood candle,
gather each strand you recall
and the blue pen, like a needle.
Suture what you can.

I. Portals

. . . where the unthinkable happens

A Lone Bird, Balanced

Riff after riff cascades from a cottonwood—
too bad nobody here speaks Bird anymore.

Oh, for a madcap diva in peacock blue,
her feathered train a ladder of eyes.
Give her a voice that breathes out honey
and arias warm as the primal yawn:
praise unfurled, wingspan wide . . .

Or summon an earnest, mustachioed tenor
whose cedary timbre makes us believe
taproots bebop under our feet,
desert hyacinth bulbs groove, beneath dunes,
while sea wind composes its chorus of stones.

Where is that diva now?
We want a translation for sky
unscrolling this endless score.
And we call for a thousand Bocelli birds
singing acres of wind and cloud
with the breadth of a robe, fallen open.

Exposed

So why do I always spot the homely birds?

Mouse-brown, on those twig feet
you look like a refugee. Are you hurt,
little wife? Are you brooding, as I am,
over the latest spill of blood and feathers,
songless, over the next ravaged nest?

Talk to me. Creak open a pocket-lined wing
concealing a cottontail, a collapsible hat.

Convince me the song of Zion lives, before
the long blue eye of this wind impels us
to shelter where doubt builds its house:
a tatter of leaves,
dust, and greenstick fractures.

She Can Only Try to Compose Herself

The wood thrush at dusk echoes
every day's hope,

each note a psalm of a self,
a white blossom

where rests fall between sounds
like petals. See the way air

cups a face that it loves, and light
strikes the hollow

curve of the throat, leaving it
speechless.

She Calls Him Dreamer

They both sign up for "Reading the Land."
He is the summit she fails to map,
a soul built for switchbacks, a seeker
of wind-shaved stone. He straddles
the ridge, beckoning.
                              She's his Wild Beauty,
but also answers to Bean, a Great Plains girl,
calm as horizon, a hill unmade.
Sometimes she thinks his veins churn
with glacial silt, clouding his gaze.
"Piece of cake," he calls.
                              Stalling
over red laces, extra-long, she criss-crosses
the loose ends on her shins like a dancer,
hoists her frameless Day-Glo-orange pack,
sagging beneath the old Dacron bag,
strapped on,
                    tight as a budget.
Eerie sounds drown out Dreamer's instructions.
Bean slow-pivots the compass points. Upwelling
water re-lacquers the lake's face, new ice
flexing against older layers, a moan,
as if a girl were
                        trapped beneath.
A dirt-brown bird with fidgets cracks its joke,
like a cocklebur. Eyeing the heights,
she ponders a dozen ways to leave,
cradles a she-cone, each small wing
hopeful as any waving hand.

Next Breath, Best Breath

For starters, don't call it a cage,
corralling the breath. Savvy fingertips
mutely Braille two dozen ribs,
each commandeering its own space
24–7, salaaming and shifting,
then rising. *Selah-h-h . . .*

Next, re-envision those lungs
as an inner atlas:
    one hundred routes
    funneling
    into branch lines,
    cloverleafs,
    cul de sacs.
Wild as papyrus, they might be
a psalter. A Rorschach. A centerfold.

Or call them dual panniers
    flanking a breastbone,
an albino koi kissing a mirror,
    all lips and flared silk.

Now, boneless as a cat at rest,
inhabit that next inhale, discerning
how spacious a backbone can be,
freeing shoulders to roll, the head to loll
and lift, floating into place: the body
aligned, alight, a home for the holy.

Blue as Devotion

Some love this world like a secret,
a promise, a sacred tease:
500 shades of blue—sea glass or sky,
sapphire, jade, night. Cool hues
play the rogue, retreat from our squint
while *come-hithering*, luminous
as the quiet splice of shadows and twilight,
fickle as evening tide's invocation
and benediction.

How many ways can one soul taste
what perfumes the mind,
be it nutmeg, narcissus, rain?
Scent, you are memory's journey mate.
Time frays, like next week's vapor trail,
the past unspools, and earth lovers
pause, gazing upward.

Jealous

Morning, with your pillowed hands
twisting over the bed, do you envy
human desire, its midnight hinge,
covet our slack-jawed alpha waves
morphing to REM and then
a prance of neurons, an in-burst
of the invisible? All those covert
sleep spindles slowing the heart,
cooling the body—yes, we are
lapped 'round with rest: one delta
astride a deepening river, one dream
richer than silt.
                    Poor Great *Ante Meridiem!*
Another graveyard shift, the looping,
half-world commute—no wonder
you snap the shade on its roller,
muttering, headboard to folded quilt,
that this life-size space we share is our first
and final host;
                    you rise alone.
And we bend, drawing the linens smooth,
makers of beds moving in tandem
toward that omega breath, unfazed,
plumped and glowing,
skins fragrant as June, tattooed
with our storied nights—oh, to be taken in
again and again and then, limp, fading,
folded away: two prayer flags, unpegged.

Warning

Think twice before trusting the generous
cottonwood tree, with its quicksilver sheen,
big-hearted leaves and their wind-sourced
repertoire: page rustle to patter of rain,
applause to downpour.
                            A tree so genial
to the hunting owl
                    will drop
                                without warning
a lushly upholstered limb,
                            smash all in its path
in that relentless way meddlers
lob hints and insinuations, leave the crater
to slowly scar over, but not before
something with talons digs in, claiming
the tree no longer a fort, a mother, a lullaby.

Darkness Muscles between Us

1
Doubt spreads its chill
like a Venetian canal at dusk:
essence of moss and rat,
sea wall frescoed with mold.

Once, we were two oars
propelling the craft of praise,
celebrants, always
down front, in God's extra houses;

now, questions ripple outward
and mouths, those ancient waterways,
amplify everything. Slow dissolves abound,
sad as the creak of wood over black water.

2
Over the gunwale, into the storm,
two feet, shoeless as prayer.

3
Boatmen of night, do you still
sing out over the starless maze
where Old World alleys converge,
where the first cry proclaims right-of-way?

There are two journeys,
ten thousand maps, one sea.
We are not lost. Go, as you must,

only say you still see me, love,
sustaining tradition, our skiff
lit by a votive's flicker: hope,
bearing an eye in a glass jar.

De Profundis

Poor sand dollars—
low tide and pillaged by gulls
on a jag—every shell
beached. Raw,

as we are. Shaped for the breath,
edges have slits
fine as buttonholes.
Noonday's stun of beaks
collapse the central star,

and five tiny doves
fall from its heart, as if
pieces of heaven
salt this desolate shore.

Torn, yet tacking
my haphazard way
through the incoming chop,
come, let me be
an ark for your sorrow.

Reflex murmurs a new name
for those who hold open
a space for another, each
entrusted with God's silence.

Tethers

It's a weird eulogy, everyone eyeing
the big red kite with its cargo of ashes,
the balding preacher in sandals
and macramé belt.

"Glory be," he says, "for a steady wind.
Today our favorite hitchhiker
rides shotgun with silk. And folks,
this is one strong mother kite."

Dreamer's eyes roll.
What follows death no longer
a sure thing for him, Bean hopes
to God her faith carries them,

praying: Please, little tin of remains
with that cunning trapdoor
and chaste dust, shaken off
by the spirit, heaven-bound,

may we all meet one day, in the air.
Until then we below are but tissue
stretched over sticks,
all our prayers, reels of string.

Crash

Hit-and-run confetti of glass,
splintered pews, sanctuary ravaged
by one kamikaze car—this could be you
and me, since your faith crashed.
We lurch through the ruins, hunting
what can be salvaged, unsure
how to rebuild. I dread
one of us four-wheeling
through our vow, splitting
the scene.

A building is fixable,
church members say,
glad that no one was hurt, except
maybe the driver, still at large—
someone else to pray for.

Whosoever opens
the *Morning Chronicle* finds
fidelity rarely makes news, although
the church's response today sidles up
to recipes on page twenty-eight,
new ways of breaking
that next loaf of bread,
generating life,
whereby
the unthinkable happens.

Burial at Sea

Salt-stung mist and wheeling gulls,
the dead first mate
trussed in his hammock of sailcloth
by seven arm-lengths of hemp
threading a whalebone needle—
talk about nightmares!
Even the corpse is sutured,
right through the nose. Cinch of knots
and weights, the hoisted cocoon's
ker-splash, colonnades of bubbles,
foam, then the sucking silence.
Sweat curdles on face and thigh,
jolting Bean awake. She reaches
for Dreamer, swathed in yards of percale
but snoring, thank God.

II. Rhapsodies and Blues

. . . the secret vibrations within,
between points of landing

Instrumental

What best engages
most of the mind is playing music.

Morning, and another blue funk
    blears the minstrel's lip and ear,
that sinuous matrix of neural stars.
    Longing plays the edges.
Zeal can be coaxed, fanned
    into shapes plated silver. Gold.

Lay it down, Dreamer,
    the way Marsalis clears a hall
of every phrase he knows
    never belonged:

Be the coiled tubing, beaded
    with vapor, the spit valve
and bell, all that keening brass
    partnering one small wind
plus three keys—mother of pearl:
    a force, bending its own mind,
inflating the pleats.

Right Brain Blues

These days, Bean drinks light,
shelves those costly oils,
her sable brush, the palette's whorls—azure
and cerulean—sky-piece hues,
left to clot. Since the surgery,
she cannot bear time vanishing, stroke
by stroke. She lives to swim
through twilight's milk, echo
birds on high, larking away,
chew the new-picked April
clover stem, four-leafed or not.
She will not mourn the scarred breast
or scenes she'll never paint, completely
here, as is. Now.

Ghost Stroke

The teacher's fingertips woo
his guitar's ebony neck, coaxing
each note's bloom, the fingerboard's
sweet, elusive moment of *give*.
Twelve strings ring
through rosewood, spruce the jaded air.

Each right-hand sweep evokes
the slap and slide-arc-caress
of a windshield blade.
To rock the groove, and he does,
bumping syncopation into our bones,
he says, "Mimic air guitar,
keeping the hand, between strums,
in motion—one breath above the strings."

Oh, for the day when our every gesture
invests know-how with warmth,
letting each pause flower, among the beats,
like journey mates tendering space,
place: to think, to breathe, leave out
the touchy exchange.

Unbelief

Begin with the body:
holy, breathing, real—how we *know*;
later, call it a book of curves,
home, riddled with contradictions.

Ask those who design, and
by design, deceive: "Which is truer,
a coin toss, or vote?
An aqueduct, or a well of salvation?
Is a seven-veil dance worth one life,
or half a kingdom?"

Or picture
Moses and Paul, head-to-head,
curled around time, two halves,
one voice, their ropey, blue-collar
topography riveting as a river
flicking a skipped stone,
as if each word cast is a net
enclosing a silver fish—arc
against air—half a second
and one small glimmer
all it takes to re-aim a skeptic's gaze.

Path Minder

Dreamer meanders
through fescue and cheatgrass,

dodging tussocks and stones,
like minor temptations,

braving the vole-holed ground
choked with knapweed—

officially noxious and
wicked on bare shins.

Illicit weeds crowd
the slender path he reopens,

and pungent stems, long after being yanked,
taint any food eaten by hand.

No matter what we've been sold, Dreamer says,
"Excising the root," like a trail fidelity blazes, in us,

"means spending time close to the earth,"
absorbing its mercurial knack

for surrender. This much can be done, daily,
unhooking the small barbed seeds from a sock.

Some Instructions on Bending

The way our barefoot yogini unfurls
   her mat suggests blue shadows:
cloudscapes flowing across snow.
   Lithe as her move into Bridge Pose,
acres of grain once swayed here—
   waves our muscles try to reanimate.
Long after Ice Age floods abated,
   long before work crews logged
their month of spring days, sanding to satin
   these planks of oak, countless
maize ballets graced this land.
   Native sowers, scythers and mothers
fed their corn to the millstone's hiss,
   then bequeathed the plow,
the shawl, the wooden bowl. Hush.
   Breathe. Integration
laves the listening ones,
   sinew to skin, sole to soul.

Washed Up

Some tunes move the foot, inside a shoe,
some elevate the soul, while others,
numinous as the song of Zion, play on
without us.
                    Remember winging it?
Fingers and toes and spirits
surrendered to more than the moment,
hearts drafting off each other,
                              daring
as swifts, weaving aerial fractals, our voices
ascending a groove, a line of thought,
into the upper reaches, then coasting
into rarified silence—the Mystery
humming within and
                        beyond all things.
No one leads the singing as you did, love.
No one else intuits my pulse
and impulse, improvising
new settings befitting
                        the inner lark.
Old friends ask about you, tender
their prayers. I am counting on this:
how greatly you're loved,
and the kingdom emerging
in guises we never knew.

En Route

Let the spiritual widow
consider stalking
our great bridges, worldwide.

Sure, a jealous wind
bullies her microphone, while
all-weather tires stutter, meeting
each sorry seam under her feet.

Despite hair lashing temples and
sticking itself to teeth and lips,
she waits, between points of landing,

recording the secret vibrations within
suspension cables. Thrumming
in chorus later, the hard-won tracks
shake her workroom, abrading

her sorrow: braided psalms of steel
suggesting an eerie
resonance, underscoring bedrock.

Here on Earth

Consider your sod, in the dead of night:
    background tick of insect feet,
        microbial choir enlivening turf,
        or an earthworm—
    five skinny hearts in a bendable straw
drilling upward, all thirst and

blind appetite, ingesting

a core sample of dirt parfait
    rich with fungi, leaf wilt and litter,
        gizzard-ground.
        Suppose that robin on late shift
    whistles, under its breath, while
stalking your moonlit yard.

Hats off to Lawn Patrol,
    first voice of the small hours:
        cheerio, cheeri-ups
        rousing the finches, who unsettle
    a scold of grackles, primed
to squabble and nosh—this could be

you, and me, digesting

all our buried
    consumptions,
        shrugging off glories
        and other things we have stolen.
    What was, still convicts us,
even in sleep.

Ms Demeanor

It all started with scissors,
and rainbow string from the Art Room,
snatched on the sly; goodbye
to my uncle's hammer and punch, looted
freely as matches and Lucky Strikes
from Irene, who never red-flagged my mother,
her purse lying wide open, it must be said;
I nicked friends and stole kisses,
swiped wooden crates for the dorm,
filched a purse, two belts, then acquired
black-and-white mug shots—yours truly on file
alongside these fingerprints; like favors
never returned, library books stacked up in corners
with pocketed change; I ripped off ideas
and heisted rock from a national park,
cheated on taxes and tithes,
gate-crashed an audition
to play the mother of Christ, go figure,
used quotes, un-cited, pirated limelight
and read on the job, still uncaught
for test answers, cribbed, and once,
a boy's innocence ran through my hands,
while for you, love, I lifted the old family beer stein;
so here's to integrity, unsullied by living
with me: little magpie, schemer, sneak,
and here's to glory, light-fingered
and offering paradise that nails me
now, red-handed and not sorry, no—
relieved, to lose my touch.

Pipe Dream

And just like that, west wind-fresh,
childhood—an August zephyr
fluting the open throats
of steel pipes, upholding a dock.
Every kid needs a hero, a little magic,
a redwood path over water.

One cannot re-pose a mother's limbs,
summer-slick with oil,
or douse a father's ire, rolled tight
as cigars in their hinged wooden box.

One dares not reenact, today,
those silences—stark or stinging
and long as a week; sometimes
quick and wicked,

a blue gill's strike,
nipping sunburned toes.
Hope dangled most of its youth
off the end of that dock.

Even now, a handful of pea gravel,
funneled into those pipes, on a whitecap-wild
windy day, alters
the pitch, each galvanized chalice
responsive as crystal meeting a fingertip:
memory, circling a wet rim.

In Defense of the Occasional Gale

Listen, in a world without wind
who'd dream of flying? Grounded,
every wing and wheel, no more kites,
gone too, vapor trails, fireworks, respirators,
our gassier verbs, like filibuster, whoop and fizzle.
Imagine all music, left unsounded. Un-mourned,
underneath the newly waveless seas, those whales
we've yet to save would never breach or spout
or serenade the secret deeps—an ocean, barely
alive to the eye. And delete Marilyn's skirt,
a Kansas farmhouse whirling toward Oz,
nightingale choirs, pollination, everyday
mutts, jowl-blown in speeding pickups.
Retire the Beaufort scale, regattas,
and plucky forecasters of weather.
Behold the Sacred Dow; see it
plunge. No use transplanting
cottonwood trees, no reason
to light that Havana cigar.
Evolution blue-pencils
beaks, tongues, lungs,
senses, limbs—lest,
with every utterance
stillborn in throats,
survivors be left
mouthing: End
of all ends,
oh, world,
without
wind.

In Thailand the Air Didn't Move

The moon was a ripe persimmon
floating above the tamarind trees.
Today, for the first time we eat one.

Call it the Ruth card,
why I signed on for Asia,
my *wither* and *goest* in earnest.
Adventure called; you longed
to inspire one dusty village,

where we learn a hundred ways to fail
the world's far side.
Sticky nights, we hold each other, fused
in misery—floor-swarm of ants,
nightly yelp of the bathroom lizard.

And one day, zeal's white flag.
The long disquiet. Debriefing.
A shrug. In hindsight,
an early signpost, marking
the long silk road of your disillusion.

Now, you don't seem to notice
I've swallowed part of a seed,
or my inclination to plant myself
in the backyard, become a tree.

Go, as you must, vagabond boy,
see the world. But first,
here's to the heart of goodness—
two youthful cynics tasting
persimmon, Far East emblem

of aging well: fruit like a fist,
then the measured
sweetening.

The Back Forty

Bean thinks about things, while walking—
like the number forty:

Pat Tillman's retired red jersey
or winks in a power nap,
the Bible's wilderness days of temptation,
direct dial code for Romania,
full-time work, the days of Lent,

not to mention the negative point
where Fahrenheit matches Celsius,

or Venus in retrograde,
and the Nebra Sky Disk—forty perforations
rimming a Bronze Age timepiece, as if
the ancients wearied of notching sticks
to reckon the wonder of each solar year,

and the fetus, turning, in watery silence,

Noah, bending before the rain,
and later, one green sprig in a beak—

or, egg to old age, the life spans
of Monarchs, drones, those fruit flies
barnstorming the bowl of peaches,

and what about forty years
of sandals slapping the Sinai sands,
and skybread, and walking out Torah,

or the average life of the lumbering hippo
and Asian elephant, the lion
and bare-eyed cockatoo?—

and now, forty years together:
wild, savory, perilous, graced.

III. Everyday Incarnations

... where what can be known expands:
fireworks, between two worlds

Wayward

Dear buck fawn, Dreamer is leaving again.
Early moon poses tonight
    inside the upturned claw of the apple tree,
Every bough glyphed with lichens,
    pewter and gold, except where antlers
Rub against bark, shedding velvet
    like youthful ideas, no longer believed.

Please, lover of apples, remind us all
    how to drink from a spring:
Angle neck to kiss an imperfect reflection.
Reach, letting every spot slide off, until
Knees dip. Wade in.

Taffy and Cold Feet

Water and salt and one long massage
romances butter, sugar and syrup
between greased palms—stretch
and fold, over and over—aerating
hot sinew. Pulled to satin,
the whole sticky mess pales
and cools, like an old wrong
muffled within a twist of torn paper.

Stories rub shoulders. I could have
pled flu, that last night in Rome,
folded, into the doorman's palm,
a few pastel lire. A note. Instead,
a no-show. Silence. So this is age:
one by one, the small derelictions.
Heat flushes up from the stove,
slipper soles worn to paper, and
underfoot, gravel.

Delicate Arch

Moab, Utah

Tendons crackle, bracing ankles
and cranky knees. Spines
curl against cold. Over the slickrock
Dreamer ventures, unaware
his wife's body presses into the cliff,
like a lost creature embedding itself,
squint-eyed, sad, yet she sees
that sandstone is performance art—
the fabled, hardscrabble arch
raveling the desert gale,
this dying light.

"I want to catch sunset," he calls, waving
his camera, forgetting Bean's fear
of thin air as ascent ends
on a ledge, owned by the wind at twilight.

A faint pressure—even gloved,
her wedding ring with its treble clef,
off-center, imprints her skin, and she twists
the gold back into its groove,
takes a mental picture: backlit
by artful erosion, the beloved body.
Linking hands, they head back down,
in deepening gloom. Weight shifts
to heels, steps slow. Her relief
airborne, with eons of dust,
shimmies among the indifferent cliffs.

Far and Away

Balloon-throat amphibians
raise their bells-on-a-harness chorus,
luscious with lust. One froglet,
suction-cupped to a stone,
shrills near my instep and then
goes mum. Like a toggle, flipped,
they all sign off.

Who will hold my hand in bed
this summer, ask about my dreams,
care how I slept?
Away is one word, vibrating
between us—dried rattle of cattails,
final as blades.

The last wave I picture is yours,
off to work in the mountains,
another idealist, headed for paradise,
and every weekend, another summit,
while I tend a century-old apple tree,
a few limbs still supple with buds.

And if I lose you . . .

Moss, they say, grows without roots,
buffers the feet on a distant crag,
velvets the struggling apple bough.

Green spell of lichen,
spring peepers, slaked, drowsing,
and you, antiphon to my psalm—
as if *a-way* is two words, after all,
as we wake, bodies amening again,
again, this joy we were shaped for.

Bear

When the neighbor tumbled all
those late-summer pears, slated for canning,
from polka dot apron to woodshed gunnysack,
she never expected

the transient, standing among her dahlias
in his rough brown coat,
grizzled whiskers clotted with juice.
She says his gold-flecked eyes
peered through her window,
examined her soapy hands and
damp curve of neck as she bowed
over the sink, where she froze, feeling
boneless, entranced, naive as a girl.

And what do we make of this?
Trembling, she untied her apron,
like caution—that prim template
we lay over chaos—
and, bent on saving her pears,
shooed him away. I say

she stepped toward ripening light
where what can be known
expands. Like Eve, re-embracing
the old sweet hazards of being,
she beheld the improbable:
honeyed claws did not rip her sack,
not a single tear.

Hunger's Plate of Secrets: Act I

Wild salmon, greens
and rosemary potatoes—

their feast almost muffles
the serrated scrape of resentment,
like knives on ironstone.

Factor in fear and hurt
with time's slow etch—no wonder
they call it crazing when
porcelain's gleaming surface
breaks down, the inroads graying,
finally immune to suds, and vigor
propelling the emery sponge.

And then there's the loaf, a tearing
and afterward, the merest
brush of hands, in passing:

"You take the heel."
"No, you. I insist."

Reading Alone at Night

And here's to the woman rightly afraid
of polar bears,
along with her Inuit sled dog, Charlie,
an intrepid twosome braving
miles of sea ice and serial blizzards,
feeding on kibbles, butter and nuts, rice
and desire, to reach that elliptical,
ever-moving magnetic North—
like long-term love, more a concept of place
than a fixed destination.

For Bean, tundra is a state of mind
where night-thoughts race. An avalanche
hammers the one she loves, miles away.
Dread cues the monster under her bed:
infidelity's fur and claws.

Eyes wide, she re-summons
glacier-deep trust, calls this a risk,
retaken, with no need to earn
this long-distance gift. She welcomes
the code yet to be cracked—
lodestone and storm: marriage.

Storm Toads: an Oracle

Womb of sand, we love you but long for rain,
and our dream of ever-after teems with fairy shrimp.

Are toads opposed to cross-species love?
No, here's to life, long as the wet world lasts.

Forget about princes, zippering out of their skins;
behold these tongues, trolling for flies! And talk about

peepers: Our eyes are vernal pools, fringed with mint,
rip-van-winkling through a two-year drought.

Who else carries the moon tucked under his chin?
Self-buoyed, we bleat our songs of love. Touch us,

and you carry our scent; then, rub your eyes in disbelief
and you could go blind—for an hour, a year.

Please believe: Toads have no cures, no crowns,
no wishes to grant. We are a spell that will not be broken.

Earthworks 301

Such dubious tutors:
the upwardly mobile drone
whose instinct sinks his career
with a single sting;

the flim-flam deer tick, upended,
six legs waving, with two new ones,
due to emerge, nose-hair thin, until
sated, it self-destructs;

the fly wannabe—that bottom crawler
and pond bum—the caddis worm, sheathed
with twiglets, rotted sedge, an earring back,
a long-gone snail's bivalve casket.

As it was in the beginning,
always the sharp hunger of fear,
then the eating, the hiding.
Note to self: when the test comes around

again, brave communion:
sip the juice,
nibble the Host nicely, and live
to claim, at last, summer's wings.

Beloved Raptor

Let the owls of Orion be wholly given
to joy, Wing-maker decrees, and to editing
voles, moles, and other tunnel junkies.

Talons gather a small brown nape
like the mouth of a drawstring purse,
night eyes and appetite serving
the Order of Things, sacral knobs of bone
picked clean as pearls, laid out in the grass
tomorrow—a sad little garden equation
yet to be parsed, a skeletal liturgy
humming: *It's still good.*

Nosing beneath my ribs, a complaint,
an appeal, blunt as the rodent's nose:
Couldn't the Rules be less harsh
for the cheeky riffraff
doing its work? Mea culpa,
I need to atone for gopher bombs,
little tampons of death
I once pushed under earth's skirt.

Seized by regret, it's hard to rise
in the dark, become a prayer.
Golden beak of heaven,
here is my heart.

Where the Sky Opens

At Sea World, will Dreamer remember?—
the trainer barebacks that killer whale,
her neoprened knees a vise.
Two creatures submerge, as one,
then breach, rocketing skyward,
a blitz of liquid silver and aquamarines,
scattering, like a broken choker.

Whose throat doesn't swell every time
perfection marries daring—her swan dive
off that treacherous nose! Glory
christens the crowd, as if atoms
left over from Paradise throb on, as if
old Adam arose, then fell
again. Naming us all.

And who can forget Eden, glimpsed?—
or how, for every gesture ascent makes,
the heart ignites a strobe, a Roman candle,
a diadem.

One prayer to agree on:
in the name of their first whale,
    may they transcend gravity,
    leap—fireworks, between two worlds.

Jonah's Whale Addresses the Almighty

Ruler of oceans, who can fathom
your summons? Pity my moans,
this small throat aching for everyday air.
Doubts are lice. They eat into brain and heart.
With a word, I'm consigned to an unknown shore.
Oh, maker of magnificent tails, reconsider
stranding me, far from the circle of my kind!
By your gift, salt is my song; your call
unleashes this sonar lament.

Never mind. You command my breath, as ever,
so let the columns of bubbles
rise, like prayers, our net
to enfold a wayward son. I'll do as I'm told, only
ease the lung-numbing gulp, the intestinal hell.
Then, may whatever end you design
close its mouth over me.
Not to leap, not to swim—but this I ask—
let me sink into you, before beaching.

IV. Tree, Temple, Wing

. . . the place each one falls

Lauds in a Pocket

More alive than your average giant,
the backyard pine rocks with song.
Blackbirds, four-and-twenty? Yes,
and No: we're talking hundreds.

Bronze needles whirly-gig down,
cabled roots creak like halyards
beneath twenty leagues of sky, the day
trilled so raptly by gleaming beaks
that one expects hymns, fanfares—
not this racket.

Curiosity reels you in: Imagine
this black-robed choir launches, as one,
and the tree weighs anchor, dragging
its mile of taproot and ivory mesh,
ground roots afloat like rigging . . .

A passing semi spits gravel,
the roosting birds jumpstart
migration: a thousand reckless
arpeggios, iridescing across the dawn.
Pocket a feather, stride home.

Re: Union

Bean can't stop bringing the meadow home
on her clothing. Barbs scratch a thigh,
thorns of cheatgrass
skewer her shoes: ingenious,
annoying life, on the move.

With each reunion, at a new motel,
rendezvous reunites them, until
her secret hope opens its trench coat
and underneath there is only
the old recognition, her prayers will not tame
him: restive, curious, born to rove.

Pluck another small burr from the pants,
break off the snagged threads.

So many points of departure
between them, all the little rifts
that temperament, taste and habit beget,
even their bodies quietly rife
with cells, coming and going, constant
as they are, in covenant, vow, friendship.

Like seeds thumbing a ride,
today she slips into the hope of becoming
transplantable. She asks for an angel
armed with a pocket spade, rending,
tending the place each one falls.

I Try to Forgive Your Absence, Facing the Snake in the Kitchen

I mistake it for a crawler, which recalls my father forcing one into jumpy nine-year-old palms so that I could ruche its long succulence onto a hook. But this one, the color of giblets, spans two checkerboard tiles and looks stunned, as I am: *How'd I end up here?* A whiplash tongue tastes the air. No Brother Francis, I swallow fear and loathing, seize Tupperware, and then, stifling dry heaves (*En garde!*) poise bin over reptile—which thrashes into spitfire life, sidewinding into the living room, all snap and writhe. A montage of past insults replays the *Why me?* refrain: A bat's webby crepe sonars over our canopy bed, five baby mice erupt from stove burner coils—how dare the creatures belie the trusty idiom "safe as houses"—each scene increasing the horror, urging murder (weight trap with soup pot, toss corpse in the morning). Outside, in the generous dark, sweaty hands press panic against plastic. Then open. Set the self free.

Yes

I am going to start living
larger, looser—
stripped down
to my sapling self, leaning toward
that leafless tree Messiah loved
enough to die on.

Maybe its boughs sheltered him once,
from pelting rain,
spread shade like a cloak,
dropped one late fig, surprising his palm—
one small story uniting and
easing them both
at the end, on that hill like a skull.

My brow touches the earth.
Moved by hosannas, echoing
still, deep inside stones,
I rise. Then the tight turn,
lifting fingers, limbs,
my bird-soft hair—
all the thorns, delicately removed.

Sunday Shoes

And now her foot's asleep. How
awkward, like trying to pull one hair
off her tongue when she's asked
to pray. Bean didn't mean to be dough
in the pew's velvet seat,
          nicely bored
waiting   waiting,
her dance card, a blank. Swaying,
she stands for the hymn, opens her throat,
and ten toes tingle awake—it's a tango
only she can hear: "Shoes,
Somebody loves you." She trembles
inside, in the quiet way
wallflowers open in simple light.

Love and Apostasy

No lightning bolt answers
your choices these days.
Instead, a growing blindness
exposes theology—strict as the slit
of a scalpel. My love, it is I,
skewed by a growing cataract,
whose pupil and retina splinter
all oncoming light.
                Dear God,
the impossible trust
I must muster, the sterile
draping of face, save
this defect—how will I ever
lie still enough?
                Prayerless,
your hand squeezes mine, having
survived this surgery, twice,
and, as sedation takes hold, you
believe I will see.

Picasso Might Have Seen It Like This

In panes, the ice glides downstream:
Below the bridge
                    our reflections collide,
pallid, broken,
                  a quarrel of edges. You,
convinced of what cannot be pieced,
slouch against the rail, at ease
in the thickening chill. Around us,
the light shunts through red cedars. How long
until the mist settles, pitching its silver tent
for the soul? I try to imagine simpler
lives, beating on beneath us: protozoa
like paisley rain,
                  lethargic with cold,
and mire, rife with reptilian dreams. Soon
the mosses will yawn, making love
with delicate cups and stems,
once the stones warm. For now,
amid this river's shifting lights,
breaking apart—how strange it is,
to feel borne along
                    on an undertow that ever
                    divides, and moves beyond.

In the Hothouse

All these small infidelities—courting
a whim, vetting the old habit—why not
the head gardener with his green thumb,
undressing Bean beside the begonias?
He steps her way,
                        she pockets her ring:
Beyond walls of glass, the Joshua trees
minutely adjust their flower canals,
co-evolvement getting it on, hustling
that next consort, the moon-loving
yucca moth, patty-caker of pollen,
embedder of eggs
to be laid like a pearl in the ripe lap
of another plant's bloom.
                            Hands touch
over a fuzzy leaf: "Cleopatra," or maybe
it's "Rex begonia." Glancing up,
the scene blurs as Bean pictures
moths, in nocturnal frenzy: skinny legs
and larval appetite.
                        So much for mystique.
Conscience, schooled by botany
with its endless, messy,
                        encroaching desire,
sees the leaf, at hand—snaps it off.

Suicide Trees

From inside out, this thriving elm
snuffs its own cells; cortex
thickens, branches spread.
Crush a leaf, and it weeps.

Some say walls around a heart
can't heal, although
harvested bark yields spices,
fibers, medicines,
resins—death, every minute,

brings gifts. A man
bathes his dying mother's feet,
cupped layers of skin, coming
away—and more than that—
adhere to his dripping hands.

When bark fails, no elm survives.
Stored in those leaves, the light
ebbs, and the used rain
passes away.

Return Engagement

With thanks to the Irvine Ranch Conservancy

Come back, refugee cactus wrens,
with your reedy, one-note chorus:
cha-char, cha-charrr. Test drive
our latest eco-brainwave,
high desert thickets of PVC cacti
hectic with needles and wire:
home sweet chollas, nine feet tall—
vinyl mea culpas. They creak,
and yes, they look like robots gone bad.

Please, little birds who love thorns,
while covert iPods air your song,
return with ribbons of litter and
brave the unknown to build
those multiple decoy nests
so that this time, the real ones
prosper, and make us ponder
what we fake, and why
what we return to, saves us.

Long Memories

Junipers siphon
               water through rock
in a rainless time.
                 One epic taproot
exploits its own
encoded genius,
               self-prunes limbs
and sloughs skin,
               redefining
grotesque. Seems
a dire climate deepens
                    interior life.
               Smoke-blue,
berries attract light,
catch a scrub jay's eye,
                  another saver
collecting tomorrows,
                  cagey with its cache.
Daily dredging want:
                this is survival,
bold as desert bones.

Catching Fire: Notes to a Raku Vase

The body of clay, like Eve, cannot
foresee raiment—be it glaze
or pelts—a fusion of itch and
ease, the grit of oneness. In the kiln,
fuel partners air, their conversation
an ongoing risk: things turning molten,
fissures, explosions.
                         "Kill the burner,"
the potter cries, manning tongs.
Tell someone you love that you lied and
watch their eyes: Even small betrayals,
coming to light with their trademark kiss,
sear, etching sheen.
                         But take the plunge—
shock of sawdust, stifle of lid—and yes,
flames crackle the glaze; it begins
along the lip. Smoke chars.
Forgiveness needs to steep, not unlike
bone ash, borate and Cornwall stone, which,
given time to cool, undisturbed, embraces
the oxides, cheek-to-cheek.
                         Voila!
Chemistry ripens the latent cobalt and copper.
Too porous to hold water,
raku will rasp the stoutest stems, and yet
beauty slips into the room,
scarred, brittle. Still breathing.

V. Segue

. . . a system poised to tip

Conclusions

Dreamer and Bean are still
sleeping apart.
Fog swarms the aspen boles.
Blurred as a backward glance,
catkins offer their wool to rime,
while two leaves, skeletons showing,
unscroll from a branch. The dream
they're both having tonight
widens its shaft, their hearts
thin as birch bark.
              Waking,
she asks old Jack
to rouse dawn, first slant of light
loosening frost like moths:
a flurry of pearled antennae,
wings, a waft of confetti—
something to warm them,
long-distance, permission
to ride the downdraft
together, through calligraphic twigs
eloquent as the turn in a story,
chalked against new sky.

Hunger's Plate of Secrets: Act II

You ask for bread. Between us
this extra virgin oil, the ruptured
garlic and clots of balsamic—
any marriage invites agitation:
flavors converse, clash.

Tonight, you say grace,
and a dawning wonder
seats itself at our table.

I, who swore off gluten, slowly
revert, eager to erase an error,
the Sunday wife, dropping her crumbs:
"Coming to church? Shouldn't we
pray? Will we ever agree on God?"

Strung Out

Treble clef power lines,
the sullen wilt of crows—
ragged, tuneless, killing time:
poets charm their birds, sound
by sound, find the familiar song
we've never heard.

What if I'm more akin
to big city fowl?
Attila the Hun seagulls
lure our tender songbirds
straight into high-rise windows,
then gorge on the fallen.

Good to remember
Noah's dove offered up
her beak and claws. I want
to be patient. Creative. Still,
foreboding beats, like a drum,
this glass heart, as if it had bones.

Every hurt place she begins to name

swells, then grows fingers
inside Bean's chest, where ribbons of sinew,
strung through her ribs, bend to pressure
approaching vibrato.
                    If she were a cellist,
she'd tighten her bow. No need to invoke Luck.
One glassy cake of rosin finesses the perfect
bite and slide:
                To accompany thoughts of ascent,
now she inhabits the cello's pose, lets fingers hover,
time, suspend—a ragged little moment—
like her first dream in another language: displacement
embraced, gently embodied.
                     Impulse cocks a wrist,
utters its prayers to pegs and bridge and scroll,
awaits the Maestro's nod, in case,
between phrases, a pause dazzles:
the shared gaze in a three-way mirror.

Every Longing Implies a Beyond

After countless summits,
a man no longer takes
weather personally.
Over time, he becomes pure
sojourn.

Picture a twisted juniper fence
where long, clear sutures of rain
needle the snags, drill into duff—
a wilderness, where thunderheads
rule, heal, kill.

Replay the big freeze,
eons of thaw and slump, flood,
upheaval. Stratified glories.
Retreat, advance, leave behind
salt . . . stone . . . sand.

Keep watch at the rim,
where soul and sky together
keep silence, another odd couple
absorbing an ancient irony:
time, in the shape of a canyon.

In the rock are invitations,
razored open to rain by roots.
Ice widens fissures, soil collects.
A juniper seed, jay-dropped,
finally settles.

Altar

The mind knows something is ending
and shakes down its cuffs,
distrusting Chance, palming its coins,
a knotted rainbow of scarves.

No sir, the mind takes itself for a stroll
among various names it knows
for spring:

Where the sodden mulleins loom,
muddling last year's path like dreams
deferred, silver rosettes burgeon,
ready their stems like bayonets;

runes of duckweed graffiti the pond
where reeds let go, lattice the muck
like a sunken basket. The mind broods.

Stump in a glade presents a table:
Let a fallen acorn and leaf
and the mottled, broken egg
stand in for the host, the plate and cup.

Solitude offers its view
of nothing more to be proved, while
Providence beckons, invoking
hosannas, palms raised.

Beginnings

One prayer smolders
tonight: a tendril
pale as smoke, tasting the air.

Once, you unfolded for me
the lace cloth, gravely placed
a beeswax candle beside
the rose, romancing McDonald's.

Now imagination suggests
heaven's marriage feast,
and, engraved with your name,
the chair I'd mentally cleared away.

Forgive me later,
when it makes sense. For now,
I'm saving a place for you,

as one day, you may for me,
when death reveals all
our puny assumptions fed,
at last, like a moth to the flame.

St. Kevin's Blackbird

Outstretched in Lent, Kevin's hand
did not expect
the blackbird's egg, its speckled warmth,

new-laid, in his uplifted palm. Think prayer
as nest: an intimate travail whereby
fledgling hopes, like birds, leave behind

a kind of grave. Amen, seeming
premature, the saint-in-waiting
dovetailed faith with knuckles.

And afterward, did he save those eggshell bits,
adorn his windowsill with each goodbye
the smallest beak ever made?

He never said. Nor will he
know these hearts of ours,
more shell than shelter,

as they fissure, let in light enough
for Christ to enter. Yes,
let grief be, with every breath, a readied womb.

Migrations

Imagine a blackbird ballet,
aerial Bolshoi:
the flash mob of feathers
wheeling
      expanding
           collapsing, never
  colliding . . .
a million and more pinions,
fluid as rivers morphing to air,
a cloud, no, a system, poised to tip
and transform. This is how

we could travel
toward wholeness, heading
      up from the tropics
          or down from the tundra,
  risking death by owl
to eavesdrop on worms, and stones,
a scrub jay rehearsing its twenty calls.

As every ear and heart
heeds the innate drive—risk
and return—we discern the contours
     survival uses, another name
        for the song of Zion,
  like everything else around,
old as rhapsody, raw as blues,
always in flux: earth lovers,
flat-out winging it.

Bedrock

Basalt is an open-air reef
blotched in orange and green,
where one man scuffs against the growth
of lichen's map, outspread—
those colonies of magical bodies:
the two-in-ones.
                    An ingenious spore
fluoresced into that first pinpoint,
fully fungus now, flush to stone
as a lick of paint—a green-gold home
for its silent partner: the alga, the unseen,
churner of light into fuel.
                    Symbiosis,
how calming, his woman thinks, sidestepping
the ancient farm under their feet.
Boots aim for a sunny table of stone,
man and wife shy as two reeds recalling
love's braided splice.
                    It isn't easy—
not like it used to be. Decades later,
they envy a rock's stored heat,
its reliable surface. Beside them,
the lichens commune among themselves,
a thousand years old and still
joined, still freeing each other.

Psalm 727

Dawn rises with tattered veils,
    wafts one last breath over the pond
    like a bridal train,
    an ivory mesh that snags on reeds
    and reveals a scroll of birch,
    inked with cryptic lines.
Alas, no message for me.
My French press steeps on the sill
    and layers of steam part.
God's hand stirs
    the rest—a glimpse within
    morning's heavy glass mug
    as a long swirl of cream
    marbles through coffee,
    each fragrant cloud
    easing this ache we call *alone.*
I break it down, say it aloud: *all one,*
    whittling hurt into small sips,
    as if prayer is a little spoon,
    funneling all the unsolved
    down its warm stem,
my cup half-full, after all.

Afterward

Procrastination

Above the dashboard's dust,
overnight ice glints
with tiny scythes. A frozen reef.
Our car key rasps against glass
as we spell *w-o-w,*
the *o* circling that rock chip
we meant to fix,
where frost shears—
a wreath of arrowheads.

Domestic entropies
attract embellishment:
mold blotches the caulking;
moss rumples a corner of lawn;
below the stove, a grease-slick
fuzzes over with dog hair. Daily
patrolling perimeters, we feel
the burden of ownership
and urgency, doing one's share, until,

from the key's etch,
warmed now by a breath,
a translucent seahorse ballet
turns fissures to praise. Hard not to
marvel, and wince,
over all we try to hold at bay, missing
the little stabs of grace. Hard to feel
grateful enough, a little sad, as
the eloquent wound holds its own.

Roaming Charges

Six months past a perm,
pockets jowling her sea-green sweats
and the glint of zippers, inch-worming,
ankles to chest—the woman
who greets Dreamer and Bean
ripples all over, an elderly mermaid.

"Can you believe," she asks,
"all these shaking bottoms in spandex!"
It's a voice born of tar, and smoke,
hearing loss, and the slow wink.
A bubble of laughter escapes,
and pale hands float from her cuffs,

shoo Dreamer and Bean away,
who turn to water inside,
even now, recalling her parting charge,
words like widening rings of light,
at dusk, when the fish are rising:
"Take care. Stay together."

Notes

The epigraph is quoted from the New International Version.

"Next Breath, Best Breath" explores a beginner's understanding of The Alexander Technique.

"Darkness Muscles between Us" owes its extended metaphor to historical travel etiquette across Venetian canals.

"Some Instructions on Bending" is for Katherine DeQuilettes.

"En Route" owes its inspiration to a woman who, years ago, created music from her sound recordings of bridge suspension cables. I've been unable to find her name but thank her. Today, the Human Harp takes the enterprise further.

"Wayward" jumpstarted itself with an acrostic poem prompt: "Think of a place."

"Procrastination" was inspired by Leesa Birdsall's stunning frost photographs.

"Reading Alone at Night" as well as "Every Longing Implies a Beyond" tip their hat to the intrepid journeys of Helen Thayer, first woman to reach the magnetic North Pole.

National Parks, rife with flora and fauna that inspired many of these poems, include:

Arches National Park
Glacier National Park
Grand Tetons National Park

Joshua Tree National Park
Mount Rainier National Park
Rocky Mountain National Park
Saguaro National Park
Yellowstone National Park
Yosemite National Park

Acknowledgments

For their generous, keen-eyed insights on these poems in earlier drafts, I thank Susan Cowger and Diane Frank for discernment, encouragement, and artistry.

For unparalleled attention to detail as well as meaning, I commend and thank my editor and fellow poet, D. S. Martin.

Grateful acknowledgment is made to the editors of the following journals, in which these poems, sometimes in different form, first appeared:

13th Moon: "Strung Out," originally titled "For the Birds, with Thanks"
Abbey of the Arts: "Blue as Devotion"
Ancient Paths: "Hunger's Plate of Secrets: Act I"
Ascent: "The Back Forty"
Barrow Street: "Instrumental," originally titled "Riff 'n Cull"
Commonweal: "Jonah's Whale Addresses the Almighty"
The Cresset: "A Lone Bird, Balanced," and "Love and Apostasy," originally titled "Apostasy"
Crux: "Where the Sky Opens"
Heliotrope: "She Can Only Try to Compose Herself," originally titled "After Seeing Old Portraits, You Try to Compose Yourself"
Ilya's Honey: "Jealous," and "Long Memories"
Kimera: "Lauds in a Pocket"
Literature Today: An International Journal of Contemporary Literature: "Reading Alone at Night"
Many Mountains Moving: "Suicide Trees," originally titled "Reading the Suicide Trees"
Natural Bridge: "Storm Toads"
Perspectives: "Earthworks 301," and "Psalm 727"

Acknowledgments

Puerto del Sol: "In Defense of the Occasional Gale," and "Bear"
Potomac Review: "Picasso Might Have Seen It Like This"
Radix: "St. Kevin's Blackbird"
Rivers of Earth and Sky: Poems for the 21st Century: "Every hurt place she begins to name," originally titled "Pause: Fingerboard, Bridge"
Rock & Sling: "Bedrock," originally titled "Double Exposure"
Rough Places Plain: Poems of the Mountains: "She Calls Him Dreamer," originally titled "Rocky Mountain Passage"
Ruminate: "Tethers," and "Re: Union," and "Darkness Muscles between Us," originally titled "Venice, in the Absence of Faith"
The Mennonite: "Sunday Shoes"
Wayfarer: "Conclusions," and "Wayward"
Wild Violet: "Right Brain Blues," and "Next Breath, Best Breath," and "I Try to Forgive Your Absence, Facing the Snake in the Kitchen"
Writer Advice: "Burial at Sea"

"Lauds in My Pocket" also appeared in *The 55 Project*
"Where the Sky Opens" also appeared in *Blessing the Animals: Prayers and Ceremonies to Celebrate God's Creatures, Wild and Tame*
"Jonah's Whale Addresses the Almighty" also appeared in *Stonework* as part of a longer poem titled "In the Valley of Salt"
"Picasso Might Have Seen It Like This" also appeared in *Bodies of Water, Bodies of Flesh*, winner of the Predator Press Chapbook Prize

COLLECTIONS IN THIS SERIES INCLUDE:

Six Sundays toward a Seventh by Sydney Lea

Epitaphs for the Journey by Paul Mariani

Within This Tree of Bones by Robert Siegel

Particular Scandals by Julie L. Moore

Gold by Barbara Crooker

A Word In My Mouth by Robert Cording

Say This Prayer into the Past by Paul Willis

Scape by Luci Shaw

Conspiracy of Light by D. S. Martin

Second Sky by Tania Runyan

Remembering Jesus by John Leax

What Cannot Be Fixed by Jill Baumgaertner

Still Working It Out by Brad Davis

The Hatching of the Heart by Margo Swiss

Collage of Seoul by Jae Newman

Twisted Shapes of Light by William Jolliff

These Intricacies by Dave Harrity

Made in the USA
Coppell, TX
19 December 2020

45822236R00059